Zombie Zone

Zombie Apocalypse

by Ruth Owen

Consultant: Luke W. Boyd
Editor in Chief
Zombie Research Society
Los Angeles, California

BEARPORT
PUBLISHING

New York, New York

Credits

Cover, © Nomad Soul/Shutterstock, © Fotokita/Shutterstock, © leolintang/Shutterstock, © ArtFamily/Shutterstock, and © Melkor3D/Shutterstock; 2–3, © froe_mic/Shutterstock; 4–5, © nouskrabs/Shutterstock, © leolintang/Shutterstock, © LifetimeStock/Shutterstock, and © Y Photo Studio/Shutterstock; 6–7, © Tomislav Pinter/Shutterstock and Kim Jones; 8, © Lipskiy/Shutterstock, © Sigarru/iStock, © Catalin205/iStock, and © AndreyPopov/iStock; 9, © Mascha_Glasa/iStock and © vchal/Shutterstock; 10, © Jon Challicom/Alamy; 11, Kim Jones; 12–13, © Seregan/Shutterstock, © grafvision/Shutterstock, © vilax/Shutterstock, © Alex Kosev/Shutterstock, © Africa Studio/Shutterstock, © Oleksandr Kostiuchenko/Shutterstock, © Dmitry Naumov/Shutterstock, and © VikiVector/Shutterstock; 14–15, © onemu/Shutterstock, © Richard Cavalleri/Shutterstock, and © Igor Kovalchuk/Shutterstock; 15, © Big Talk/Wt 2/Kobal/REX/Shutterstock; 16, © digitalvox/Shutterstock, © Chanclos/Shutterstock, and © xpixel/Shutterstock; 17, © Borkin Vadim/Shutterstock, © Richard Cavalleri/Shutterstock, and © Igor Kovalchuk/Shutterstock; 18–19, Kim Jones; 20–21, © Phoric/Shutterstock, © Boris Ryanposov/Shutterstock, © Africa Studio/Shutterstock, © vilax/Shutterstock, and © Vectorpocket/Shutterstock; 22T, © leolintang/Shutterstock; 22BL, robert8/Shutterstock; 22BR (clockwise from upper left), © canbedone/Shutterstock, © Mega Pixel/Shutterstock, © Janis Smits/Shutterstock, © endeavor/Shutterstock, and © MidoSemsem/Shutterstock; 23, © Callahan/Shutterstock.

Publisher: Kenn Goin
Creative Director: Spencer Brinker
Photo Researcher: Ruth Owen Books

Library of Congress Cataloging-in-Publication Data

Names: Owen, Ruth, 1967– author.
Title: Zombie apocalypse / by Ruth Owen.
Description: New York : Bearport Publishing Company, Inc., 2018. I Series: Zombie zone I Includes bibliographical references and index.
Identifiers: LCCN 2017049029 (print) I LCCN 2017051133 (ebook) I ISBN 9781684024988 (Ebook) I ISBN 9781684024407 (library)
Subjects: LCSH: End of the world—Miscellanea—Juvenile literature. I Zombies—Juvenile literature.
Classification: LCC BF1999 (ebook) I LCC BF1999 .O93 2018 (print) I DDC 398/.45—dc23
LC record available at https://lccn.loc.gov/2017049029

For more information, write to Bearport Publishing Company, Inc., 45 West 21st Street, Suite 3B, New York, New York 10010. Printed in the United States of America.

10 9 8 7 6 5 4 3 2 1

Contents

Outbreak! 4

Day 1 – Attack!. 6

Day 2 – Zombie at My Door 8

Day 3 – Bad to Worse. 10

Day 4 – Survival Mode 12

Day 4 *continued* – Staying Safe 14

Day 5 – Escape Before Dawn! 16

Day 5 *continued* – A Place to Hide 18

Trying to Survive 20

Make a Zombie Survival Kit . . . 22

Glossary 23

Index. 24

Read More 24

Learn More Online 24

About the Author 24

Outbreak!

Could a zombie apocalypse really happen? Could the world be overrun with **hordes** of undead bodies, staggering around with one aim—to feed on living humans?

Although very unlikely, a deadly new **virus** with zombielike symptoms could appear. In such an event, the Centers for Disease Control and Prevention (CDC), a U.S. government agency, would immediately put the following emergency plan into action:

- Identify the virus causing the disease.
- Work on a cure.
- **Quarantine** the infected.

To see how one person has imagined the unfolding of such a frightening **outbreak**, take a deep breath and turn the page…

An apocalypse is a highly destructive event that leads to the deaths of millions of people.

Attack!

The nightmare started with an urgent news bulletin about people falling ill across the city. A TV reporter said the sick had high fevers and foamed at the mouth. Within hours, they were unable to walk or talk.

The reporter also described something very unexpected. Within minutes after a man with the disease had been declared dead, his **corpse** had jolted upright and began attacking the doctor—chewing the flesh off of his face.

The TV reporter looked stunned as she stared into the camera.

What was next? I wondered.

BREAKING

In addition to a virus, some people believe that a drug, a chemical, or **radiation** exposure could turn people into the walking dead.

Zombie at My Door

On the morning news, video shot from a helicopter showed hundreds of blood-spattered zombies staggering through the city's streets. Police reported that all the people in the video had been bitten and then died—before becoming the walking dead.

By nightfall, the city was overwhelmed with zombies. The air smelled of rotting flesh. One creature even banged at my door, trying to knock it down. When I looked through the **peephole**, empty yellow eyes stared back at me!

The dead thing then tried to get in through my mail slot. It broke off part of its arm and just left it hanging in my door before wandering away.

According to zombie **lore**, a zombie cannot feel pain, even when it loses a body part!

9

Bad to Worse

The government declared a **state of emergency** at 10:00 AM this morning as thousands of zombies now roamed the city. The uninfected were told to **barricade** themselves inside their homes.

As I peeked through the heavy curtains on my front window, I saw zombies in my yard! They had found a victim. They gnawed at his legs and swallowed handfuls of his **entrails**. I froze—I could be their next meal . . .

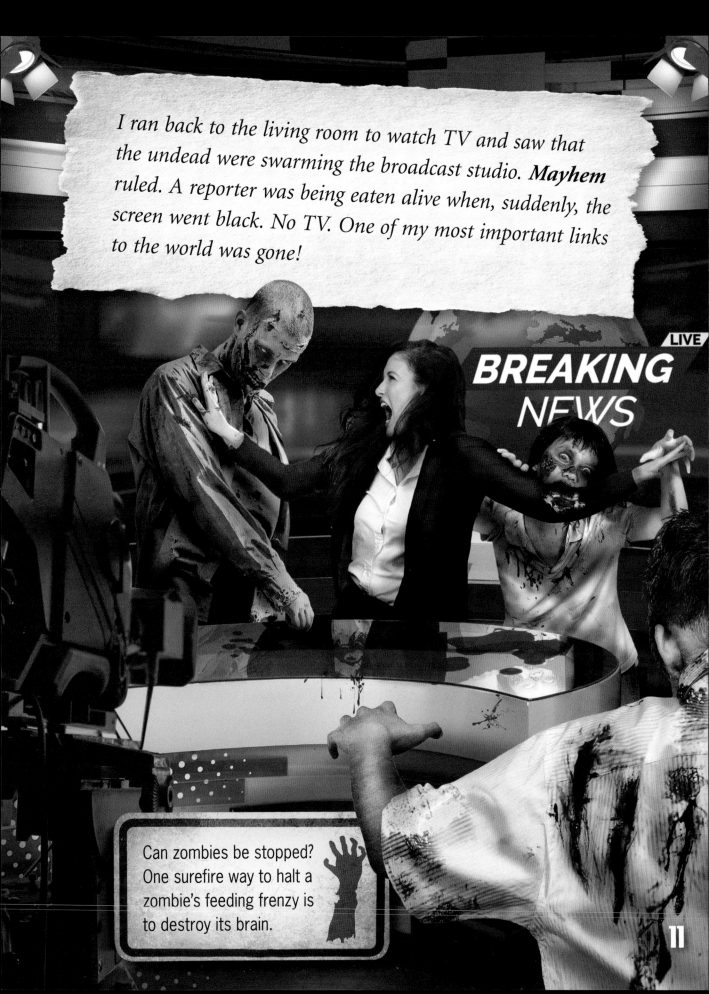

I ran back to the living room to watch TV and saw that the undead were swarming the broadcast studio. **Mayhem** ruled. A reporter was being eaten alive when, suddenly, the screen went black. No TV. One of my most important links to the world was gone!

LIVE

BREAKING NEWS

Can zombies be stopped? One surefire way to halt a zombie's feeding frenzy is to destroy its brain.

Survival Mode

After a sleepless night, I woke up to find there was still no TV. There was also no electricity or water, and my cell phone was dead. Most of the comforts of **civilization** had disappeared in little more than three days.

On my battery-powered radio, I heard reports of streets covered with the blood of zombie victims. I had no idea what to do. If I stayed in my house, I'd soon die from lack of water and food. I knew I had to run. But before I did, I needed to pack a survival kit. At the very least, it needed to include water, food, a flashlight, and batteries.

- FOOD
- WATER
- BATTERIES
-

During an apocalypse, there would be no workers to operate power plants. Without electricity, TVs, phones, and computers would not work.

Staying Safe

It's almost midnight and all the streetlights are dark. I don't see any of the creatures on my moonlit lawn or hear their awful moans. My bike is in the yard next to a tree. If I can get to it, maybe I can make a quick getaway.

To protect myself, I'm wearing jeans with a leather jacket and knee and elbow pads. I've tied a bandana over my nose and mouth to protect myself from zombie fluids. As I strap on my backpack and open my door, I tremble, knowing that a single bite would mean a horrible, painful death.

If you cannot outrun a zombie horde, do the following: Moan, groan, stagger, and shuffle so that you seem like one of them.

Escape Before Dawn!

I could never have imagined what was waiting in my yard. In the shadows, black crows pecked at human body parts. Clouds of flies filled the air like fog.

As I ran for my bike, a woman in a robe came shuffling toward me. Fat, white **maggots** slithered in and out of her nose. As she reached for me, I recognized her. She was my next-door neighbor!

I dodged her, jumped on my bike, and began to pedal hard. But where should I go? There were zombies everywhere. If I could reach a **remote** location, I might be able to survive.

A supermarket would be a good hiding place because it would be well-stocked with supplies. But it would probably be overrun with zombies looking for people to feed on!

A Place to Hide

As I pedaled away from my house in the early morning hours, I found the roads filled with stopped cars. Some were empty with their doors left wide open. Others were clearly the scene of zombie attacks—the seats covered in blood. However, as I made my way to the outskirts of the city, I saw fewer and fewer zombies. And then, I didn't see any at all.

When I spotted a gas station that looked deserted, I stopped for badly needed supplies. I grabbed water along with some food. Then I headed for the mountains. Far from the city, I hoped to hide in the thick forests and perhaps find other survivors.

Places with few people are less likely to be infected with a virus that moves from person to person. Viral **transmission** is highest in crowded areas.

Trying to Survive

As I write this, I'm sitting in a shelter made from tree branches. So far, I haven't found any other survivors. Thankfully, I haven't seen any zombies, either.

It rained shortly after I built my shelter, so I was able to catch some fresh water in a plastic bottle I had in my backpack. And I found some blackberries to eat at the edge of the forest.

After I rest for a while, I'm going to look around for other survivors. On the only radio station I can still get, I hear that the CDC has **isolated** the virus. How long will it take to develop a **vaccine**, I don't know. But until I do, I'll wait here, trying my best to survive this zombie apocalypse.

The CDC has actually produced a guide to help citizens prepare for and survive a zombie apocalypse. The agency felt it was a fun way to show people how to plan for real-life emergencies, such as hurricanes and floods. The CDC doesn't believe a zombie apocalypse could actually happen, but then how can anyone be sure?

Make a Zombie Survival Kit

If a zombie apocalypse took place, would you be one of the survivors—or one of the undead?

Imagine that hordes of zombies are rampaging through your town or city. You have been hiding out in your home, but must now escape to a safe place. You can take just one backpack of survival items with you. What would you pack?

Remember the following:

- Everything you take must already be in your home.
- All the items you choose must fit into a backpack.

1. In a notebook, make a list of at least 10 things you would pack. Write one sentence explaining why each item will be useful.

2. Put the items in order of priority. For example, if water is first and food is second, what items come next?

3. Look at the five survival kit items below. If you could take only three of them, which would you choose and why?

Compass

Duct tape

Matches

Soap

Plastic tarp

Glossary

barricade (BA-ruh-kade) to build a barrier to keep out unwanted attacks

civilization (siv-uh-luh-ZEY-shuhn) an advanced human society with a government, culture, science, and industry

corpse (KORPS) a dead body

entrails (EN-treylz) the intestines and other parts from a person's or animal's belly

hordes (HORDZ) large groups or crowds

isolated (I-so-lay-tid) separated from others

lore (LAWR) traditional beliefs and stories

maggots (MAG-uhts) the larvae, or wormlike young, of flies that often feed on dead bodies

mayhem (MAY-hem) a state of violent disorder

outbreak (OUT-brake) a sudden start of something, such as the spread of a disease

peephole (PEEP-hohl) a small hole in a door that allows a person to see outside

quarantine (KWAWR-uhn-teen) to isolate sick people from healthy people to keep a disease from spreading

radiation (ray-dee-AY-shuhn) a form of energy that can be very dangerous to the human body

remote (ri-MOHT) far from a town or city

state of emergency (STATE UHV ih-MUR-juhn-see) a time of national danger or disaster when a government puts emergency plans into action

transmission (trans-MISH-uhn) the passage of something from one person to another

vaccine (vak-SEEN) a preparation that prevents infection

virus (VYE-ruhss) a microscopic organism that infects cells and causes disease

Index

body parts 8–9, 10–11, 16
brain 11
Centers for Disease Control and Prevention (CDC) 5, 20
communication 6, 8, 11, 12–13, 20
lore 9
outbreak 4–5
quarantine 5
radiation 7
state of emergency 10
survival kit 12–13, 22
survivors 18, 20, 22
symptoms 5, 6
undead 4, 11, 22
U.S. government 5, 10, 20
vaccine 20
virus 5, 7, 19, 20
zombie horde 15

Read More

Page, Sean T. *Preparing for and Surviving the Zombie Apocalypse (Surviving Zombie Warfare)*. New York: Rosen (2016).

Wacholtz, Anthony. *Can You Survive a Zombie Apocalypse? An Interactive Doomsday Adventure (You Choose: Doomsday)*. North Mankato, MN: Capstone (2015).

Weakland, Mark. *Zombies and Forces and Motion (Monster Science)*. North Mankato, MN: Capstone (2011).

Learn More Online

To learn more about a zombie apocalypse, visit
www.bearportpublishing.com/ZombieZone

About the Author

Ruth Owen has been developing and writing children's books for more than 10 years. She lives in Cornwall, England, just minutes from the ocean. If there's a zombie apocalypse, she intends to escape by boat!